Famous
Wagon Trails

Christy Steele

WORLD ALMANAC® LIBRARY

Please visit our web site at: www.worldalmanaclibrary.com
For a free color catalog describing World Almanac® Library's list of high-quality books
and multimedia programs, call 1-800-848-2928 (USA) or 1-800-387-3178 (Canada).
World Almanac® Library's fax: (414) 332-3567.

Library of Congress Cataloging-in-Publication Data

Steele, Christy, 1970-
    Famous wagon trails / by Christy Steele.
      p. cm. — (America's westward expansion)
    Includes bibliographical references and index.
    ISBN 0-8368-5788-7 (lib. bdg.)
    ISBN 0-8368-5795-X (softcover)
    1. Frontier and pioneer life—West (U.S.)—Juvenile literature. 2. Trails—
West (U.S.)—History—Juvenile literature. 3. Overland journeys to the Pacific—
Juvenile literature. 4. West (U.S.)—History, Local—Juvenile literature. 5. West
(U.S.)—Description and travel—Juvenile literature. 6. West (U.S.)—History—
19th century—Juvenile literature. I. Title.
F596.S826   2005
978'.01—dc22   2004057822

First published in 2005 by
World Almanac® Library
330 West Olive Street, Suite 100
Milwaukee, WI 53212 USA

Copyright © 2005 by World Almanac® Library.

Produced by: EMC—The Education Matters Company
Editors: Christy Steele, Rachael Taaffe
Designer and page production: Jennifer Pfeiffer
Maps and diagrams: Jennifer Pfeiffer
World Almanac Library® editorial direction: Mark J. Sachner
World Almanac Library® art direction: Tammy West
World Almanac Library® production: Jessica Morris
World Almanac Library® editors: Monica Rausch, Carol Ryback

Photo credits: Central Pacific Railroad Photographic History Museum, © 2004, CPRR.org: 37, 40, 42, 43;
Corbis: 26; Denver Public Library Western History Collection: 4, 10, 11, 14, 15, 33, 41, 44; Library of
Congress: cover, 7, 9, 13, 16, 18, 22, 24, 28, 30, 34; North Wind Picture Archives: 6; Union Pacific
Railroad Museum: 21.

Printed in Canada

1 2 3 4 5 6 7 8 9 09 08 07 06 05

Contents

Chapter 1

The Trailblazers

I n the early 1800s, the area that
would become the western United
States was completely undeveloped.
Explorers, hunters, traders, and settlers
had to blaze their own trails. The use
of covered wagons to move possessions
and supplies became commonplace.
This era of westward expansion
spanned more than one hundred years,
from about the time of the Louisiana
Purchase in 1803 to 1912. During that
time, America grew from seventeen
states to forty-eight states.

Manifest Destiny was the belief
that Americans had a God-given right
to take over the continent. As they
moved west, settlers used this policy
to spread U.S. ideas and government
to new people and territories. To
achieve Manifest Destiny, the United
States purchased land from other
countries or conquered territory by

◀ In this undated photo taken in the 1800s, a
covered-wagon train makes its way through Ute
Pass in Colorado.

taking land from Native peoples until its borders stretched from coast to coast.

The removal of the Native Americans from their homelands opened huge expanses of land, and increasing numbers of Anglo settlers seized the opportunity to move from the East to the West and claim the land for themselves. More than one-half million people chose to travel West on trails between 1800 and 1870, forming the largest mass migration in history.

Lewis and Clark Expedition

At first, Anglo settlers from the eastern United States were fearful of moving too far West because there were no roads, trails, or maps of the area. Explorers Meriwether Lewis and William Clark changed this situation.

The Lewis and Clark Expedition (1804–1806), also known as the Corps of Discovery, was the first exploration funded by the U.S. government. President Thomas Jefferson wanted to survey U.S.-owned land recently acquired in the Louisiana Purchase in hopes of finding an easy water passage from the Mississippi northwestward to the Pacific, establishing new trading opportunities, and discovering natural resources to enrich the country.

About forty-eight men and at least one woman accompanied Lewis and Clark on their expedition to the West, and together the Corps blazed a new trail to the Pacific Ocean. They traveled for two and one-half years over land and by river, mapping about 4,000 miles (6,500 kilometers) of the terrain. Their route began near present-day Wood River, Illinois, and passed through portions of what are now Missouri, Kansas, Iowa, Nebraska, South Dakota, North Dakota, Montana, Idaho, Oregon, and Washington.

▶ This hand-colored illustration by Patrick Gosslew shows the Corps of Discovery shooting a grizzly bear, then unknown to Easterners, while exploring the Louisiana Territory. They took the grizzly's skin back to President Thomas Jefferson.

A number of the Corps's journal entries describe their encounters with the territory's animals, many of which were not yet known in the East. While crossing the Great Plains, they were attacked by grizzly bears, which the group had never seen or heard of before. The men also supplemented their food supply by hunting the region's wild game, such as buffalo, deer, and beaver. Whenever possible, the Corps captured live specimens of animals they had never seen, such as prairie dogs, and sent them back to President Jefferson. If an animal was too large or dangerous to transport, such as a grizzly bear, the group first sketched the animal before killing it, then preserved its skin or skeleton to take back East for study.

Lewis and Clark also chronicled the region's Native peoples and their customs, such as the traditional Mandan buffalo hunt. The presence of Sacajawea, a Shoshone woman who served as guide and interpreter for the Corps, helped the group communicate with different Native groups. Lewis and Clark gave gifts to Native American groups to establish friendly relations between them and the U.S. government. They also traded goods with Native peoples for food when game was not available and for horses to travel overland.

The explorers became national heroes when they arrived back home in the East. They gave talks about their travels, and their expedition journals were widely read. The route taken by Lewis and Clark, however, was not practical for mass movements of people because it was too difficult for wagons to travel it. Still, some adventurous people, armed with new maps from the Lewis and Clark Expedition, were inspired to make the journey West in search of riches.

▼ Mountain men trapped many different kinds of animals for their fur, including beavers, rabbits, raccoons, and even bears. Here, two mountain men set a trap for a bear in 1895.

Mountain Men

Mountain men were the first people to follow in Lewis and Clark's footsteps. These rugged men moved from place to place on horseback or mule and trapped animals and harvested the furs to sell. Many mountain men also traded goods with Native Americans for furs.

In the early 1800s, hats made from beaver pelts were popular with wealthy Europeans, so trapping beavers could make a mountain man a good living. Lewis and Clark had written about the many beavers they saw during their expedition, and beginning in 1807, mountain men journeyed to the Rocky Mountains in search of these beavers. Mountain men around the Upper Missouri River also hunted buffalo and traded items for buffalo robes

Jedediah Smith (1798–1831)

Jedediah Smith was one of the most daring explorers and mountain men of the West. Smith's goal was to open unexplored areas of the Southwest to settlement and trapping. He journeyed through southern Nevada in 1827, crossed the South Pass through the Rocky Mountains, and was the first to explore the Great Basin of Nevada and tell others about it. Records of his journeys helped lead settlers across difficult terrain on the route to California.

Smith described why he traded and explored in an 1829 letter to his brother: "It is that I may be able to help those who stand in need, that I face every danger. . . . It is for this, that I go for days without eating, and am pretty well satisfied if I can gather a few roots, a few snails, or, better satisfied if we can afford ourselves a piece of horse flesh, or a fine roasted dog, and most of all, it is for this, that I deprive myself of the privilege of society and the satisfaction of the converse of my friends!"

In 1831, Smith was killed by Comanche warriors while traveling the Santa Fe Trail. His body was never found.

from Native Americans.

Many mountain men usually worked for fur trading companies, such as John Jacob Astor's American Fur Company and the Rocky Mountain Fur Company. Some companies built trading posts where mountain men and Native Americans would come to sell their pelts and buy supplies. Fort Laramie on the Platte River, Fort Floyd on the Yellowstone River, Fort Bridger on the Green River, Fort Henry on the Snake River, and Bent's Fort on the Arkansas River all began as fur-company trading posts.

Other companies organized a yearly meeting, called a rendezvous, where trappers gathered to sell or trade their pelts for money and supplies. These rendezvous for mountain men could last weeks and were famous for their drinking, gambling, storytelling, and contests of skill, such as footraces, sharp shooting, or knife throwing.

During their search for furs, mountain men made new discoveries and blazed many

new trails around the West. Robert Stuart made one of the most important discoveries of the era when he found the famous South Pass of the Rocky Mountains in what is now southwestern Wyoming while on a trip to trap and establish Astoria, an Oregon trading post, in 1812. Although Stuart was first to discover the valley, his boss kept the South Pass secret because it gave his fur-trading company a traveling advantage. Mountain man Jedediah Smith rediscovered it in 1824 and publicized its existence in his letters to friends in the East.

Between 1810 and 1840, the fur trade was a booming business west of the Mississippi. By the 1840s, however, silk had replaced beaver as the preferred material for making European hats, and the fur trade began to decline. Some mountain men became professional buffalo hunters to harvest pelts and supply trading posts or army forts with food. Others became army scouts, guides, or armed escorts for the ever-increasing numbers of wagon trains traveling to the West.

▲ Native Americans and trappers around a campfire. Mountain men had friendly relations with some Indian groups in the West, including the Snake, the Crow, and the Shoshone. They often traded with these Indians. Other tribes, such as the Blackfeet, resented the presence of mountain men.

Life on a Westward Trail

After mountain men had blazed trails, people from the East began traveling on these routes to move West. The trail a settler chose depended on the family's final destination, but all trails were difficult trips that would last for several months. Each trail had its own challenges, such as mountains, river crossings, or deserts. The most popular trails were the Santa Fe Trail; the Oregon Trail; the Mormon, or Nevada, Trail; and the California Trail.

Settlers moved West for many reasons—to find adventure or work, to find gold, to claim cheap or free land, or to escape debts, religious persecution, or the law. Immigrants from Europe left their countries to escape

◀ Ezra Meeker was a farmer in western Washington in the 1880s. As a boy, he traveled the Oregon Trail with his family to reach his new home. Later in life, he erected markers along the trail and worked tirelessly to preserve it.

poverty and start fresh in the United States. Unlike mountain men who traveled from place to place, most settlers were in search of one piece of good land to claim as their own.

Covered Wagons

Settlers used wagons covered by waterproofed U-shaped cotton covers, or bonnets, to travel overland trails. The thick bonnets helped protect settlers' goods from rain, snow, or dust. On the wide-open prairie, the bonnets looked like the sails of a schooner, a type of ship. As a result, the wagons were often called "prairie schooners."

Settlers used strong wood to construct a wagon and built special storage compartments inside it to secure their possessions and supplies, which consisted of farming equipment, seeds, tools, food, clothes, livestock, eating utensils, a stove, replacement wagon parts, water barrels, guns, and ammunition.

Sometimes, all the members of a wagon train painted their wagons the same bright color for the trip or wrote their destination on their wagons' bonnets, such as "Pike's Peak or bust."

▼ As more and more people used the trails westward, the trails became more like roads. Wagon ruts developed, providing a definite route to follow, and in some places, signs were erected, such as this signpost announcing the beginning of the Wyoming Territory.

The Trail

Trails in the West were unpaved and deeply rutted by wagon wheels. The trip was dusty and so bumpy in places that milk left in the wagon in the morning would be churned into butter by evening. If it rained, wagons often got stuck in mud or sand.

The Homestead Act

On May 20, 1862, to encourage westward movement of U.S. citizens, Congress passed the Homestead Act, a liberal land grant policy that offered inexpensive or free public domain land to individual citizens in exchange for improving and farming the land. Under this law, a person could "select any surveyed land up to 160 acres (65 hectares) and to gain title to it after f ive years' residence, making prescribed improvements, and paying a modest fee for the service of the register and the receiver." The improvements required were living on the homestead, building a home, digging a well, and farming and fencing a certain portion of the land.

The Homestead Act opened 270 million acres (109 million ha), or 10 percent of the area of the United States, to settlement. Any head of household who was twenty-one years or older and was a citizen or intending to become a citizen of the United States could take advantage of the free land offered by the Homestead Act, but first they had to move West and claim the land.

The trip took a long time because most wagons were so heavily loaded with supplies that they only traveled 2 miles (3 km) an hour. Many settlers chose to walk barefoot alongside the slow-moving wagons rather than ride inside because they were so uncomfortable. With such slow wagon speeds, settlers often found themselves making camp in sight of the previous day's camp.

There were no hotels along the trail, but some trails did have a few forts and trading posts that had been established during the fur-trading years. The U.S. Army also built some forts along popular trails to protect travelers from attacks by Native American groups who were angry that Anglos had invaded their land.

The Wagon Train

Usually a few families from the same town traveled together in a wagon train made of at least several wagons. Large wagon trains could have twenty or more wagons traveling together. The group worked together to move their wagons across streams or rivers, fix broken wagons, take care of children, and forage and hunt for food along the trail.

Members of a wagon train usually elected a leader, or trail boss, who set the schedule and decided where to stop for rests and set up the evening camp. Each wagon train also made its own rules. Members had to decide, for example, whether to travel every day or to observe the Sabbath Sunday, a day that the Bible reserved for rest.

A Day on the Trail

Settlers began each day on the trail before dawn by preparing and eating a breakfast that usually consisted of coffee, bacon, beans, and dry bread. To prepare for the day's journey, the family would gather any livestock they owned, fill water barrels if near a water source, and hitch their team to the wagon. Departure time depended on the schedule the wagon train had agreed upon before departing, but most wagon trains were moving along the trail by 7 A.M.

Around noon, the wagon train would stop for a midday break. They rested as they ate cold leftovers from breakfast and were usually moving again by 2 P.M. They made evening camp

▼ Pioneers packed their wagons as tightly as they could. Even so, they sometimes had to leave their books, extra clothing, and other items along the trail in order to lighten the load for their weary mules or oxen. This 1850 illustration shows a wagon train heading to California.

around 6 P.M. Some wagon trains pulled their wagons into a "U" or circle shape at night to help them defend against wild animals, bandits, or possible attacks by Native Americans. They put their livestock in the middle of the wagons to prevent livestock from stampeding or running away.

A pioneer family eats lunch at the foot of the Rocky Mountains sometime around 1875. Crossing the Rocky Mountains was one of the most difficult parts of traveling west.

Next, they gathered wood or dried buffalo and cow manure and built a fire. The evening meal was usually simple but could include fresh meat, such as buffalo or deer, if there had been some success hunting along the trail. Some settlers went to sleep early, but others sang songs or told stories around campfires.

A few settlers slept in the wagons, but wagons were so packed with supplies that most slept in the open wrapped in blankets or on mats on the ground. Some wealthier settlers brought tents or mattresses that could be filled with air or water to make them more comfortable.

Trail Dangers

To help prepare for any possible dangers on the trip, settlers who could afford to hired mountain men as guides and guards. Guides helped make sure that settlers did not get lost along the trail. If settlers got lost, they could get stuck in the snowy mountains and run out of food before the snow thawed in spring. Guards also protected against Native American attacks, though these were rare along the trails.

Weather could cause dangers along the trail. Covered wagons offered some protection from the elements, but not much. Wagon trains could become lost or be partially buried in dust storms. Freezing temperatures, snow, and hailstones could harm settlers and their wagons and livestock. Lightning strikes could start fires on the dry prairies. Drought could make water supplies dry up so that there was nothing for settlers to drink along the trail.

On the other hand, too much water also caused problems for wagon trains. A lot of rainfall could make the water levels in rivers and creeks rise. This made river crossings especially dangerous. Sometimes, wagon trains would wait weeks, hoping for the water levels to fall. This could slow their progress enough that they were caught in snowstorms in mountain passes later on the trail. Some settlers built rafts to float their wagons across rivers.

The conditions on the trail were bad for health. Different illnesses, such as smallpox, scurvy, or typhoid, killed many people. Those who died were buried alongside the trail.

▲ Ezra Meeker caulks his wagon before a river crossing to keep out water. Rivers were a major hazard of westward travel—wagon wheels could become mired in muddy bottoms or suffer damage from rocks, and people could be carried off by swirling currents.

Chapter 3

The Santa Fe Trail

The Santa Fe Trail, one of the old-est trails in the West, began to be used in 1821 as an international west-ern trading trail between Mexico and the United States. The trail stretched for about 1,000 miles (1,609 km) from present-day western Missouri to New Mexico, which was a northern province of Mexico from 1821 until it was ceded to the United States in 1848. Hundreds of merchandise caravans traveled the Santa Fe Trail from 1821, when Mexico opened trade with the United States, until 1880 when the railroad reached Santa Fe.

Its dry desert terrain made the Santa Fe Trail one of the most danger-ous trails in the West, and thousands of people and their livestock died trav-eling it. In 1844, a merchandise caravan with a herd of two hundred

◀ Traders crossing a dry tributary of the Gila River on the Santa Fe Trail in an 1845 illustration. The Gila Trail to Mexico linked up with the Santa Fe Trail. Travelers could also take the Camino Real all the way into Mexico City.

mules was stranded without food by a blizzard. The people survived, but the poor mules ate bark and even each other's tails in an attempt to survive, but most of them died.

The Route

Travelers preparing to cross the Santa Fe Trail gathered each spring in the most westward "jumping-off" towns along the Missouri River. Travelers were good for business in these towns, and each town in the area competed to lure the most visitors by promising bargain supplies and the best living conditions. The Missouri towns of Franklin, Independence, and Westport Landing (what is now Kansas City) were among the most popular departure towns for the trail.

Once underway, wagon trains followed the north bank of the Arkansas River, slowly traveling through the prairie grass of

▼ This map shows the route of the Santa Fe Trail.

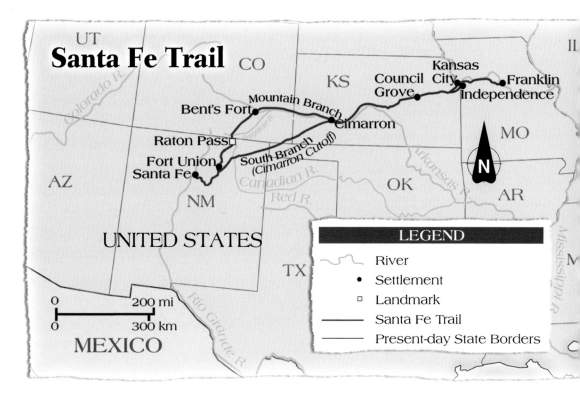

17

▶ In 1859, Daniel Jenks sketched this picture of his camp on Cottonwood Creek in eastern Kansas while traveling along the Santa Fe Trail.

Cottonwood Creek Sunday April 10th 1859

present-day Kansas. Then, about three-quarters of the way through southwestern Kansas, the route diverged into two branches—Mountain Branch or South Branch.

The longer Mountain Branch continued westward to Bent's Fort near the Purgatoire River in present-day Colorado. It then turned southwestward, and travelers had to cross the dangerous and narrow Raton Pass through the Sangre de Cristo Mountains. To get the wagons across this pass, many caravans had to unload their merchandise, disassemble the wagons, lower the goods and wagon pieces with ropes, and then reassemble and reload the wagons.

The South Branch, known as the Cimarron Cutoff, quickened the trip by angling sharply to the southwest to make the journey 100 miles (160 km) shorter. This route, in general, was easier for wagons to travel, but the cutoff still had special hazards. Caravans had to cross the Arkansas and Canadian Rivers as well as a waterless 50-mile (80-km) desert plain.

The two branches eventually converged into one trail again at the foothills of the Sangre de Cristo Mountains near Fort Union, in present-day New Mexico, and continued to Santa Fe. In good traveling conditions, the entire trip took fifty to sixty days.

History of the Trail

Portions of the Santa Fe Trail were used thousands of years before Europeans arrived. Buffalo wandered across parts of the trail, and the Native American groups who hunted these buffalo followed the buffalo's paths. Spanish explorers traveling north from present-day Mexico also used similar routes through the area, but it was not until 1821 that the trail became popularized by a trader from the United States, named William Becknell.

William Becknell, known as the "Father of the Santa Fe Trail," led the first merchandise caravan from Franklin, Missouri, to Santa Fe in 1821, after he learned that Mexico had opened to U.S. trade. The Mexicans in Santa Fe greeted his expedition's arrival with a parade and feast. Becknell set up shop around the town's central plaza, sold all of his merchandise, and returned to Franklin with a big profit.

In 1822, Becknell recruited several other traders and began his second trip to Santa Fe with three wagons, but the trip turned disastrous. Becknell felt the wagons could not cross the Raton Pass and decided to blaze the Cimarron Cutoff. On this shortcut, many of the expedition's livestock died of thirst, and the traders were forced to kill their dogs and drink the dogs' blood to stay alive. The men buried their goods, left their wagons behind, and staggered through the desert for miles until they saw a buffalo with a belly distended from recently drinking water. They killed the buffalo and drank the water from its stomach. This gave them the liquid nourishment they needed to continue moving forward until reaching water.

After Becknell's experience, wagon trains choosing the Cimarron Cutoff knew to bring extra supplies of water stored in barrels. This method worked as long as there were no unexpected delays, such as becoming lost in the featureless landscape or being stranded by bad weather, such as dust storms.

In 1824, Becknell returned to Santa Fe with eighty-one men and twenty-four wagons full of $30,000 worth of trade goods, such as hardware, cutlery, and flour. He sold his goods in Santa Fe for $180,000 in gold and silver and $10,000 in furs, earning about 600 percent profit, and then returned to Franklin in 1825.

Inspired by Becknell's success, increasing numbers of merchandise caravans began to use the Santa Fe Trail each year. In Santa Fe, traders could sell their goods or continue on to new destinations on other trails, such as the Gila Trail that went deep into Mexico or the Old Spanish Trail that crossed through what is now Utah and Nevada and ended in California.

The U.S. Government and the Santa Fe Trail

During the Mexican-American War (1846–1848), the Santa Fe Trail became an important U.S. government thoroughfare. In 1846, U.S. General Stephen Watts Kearny marched his troops along the trail and defeated a force of four thousand Mexicans and Indians at Santa Fe to assume control of New Mexico.

On October 19, 1847, General Kearny ordered a battalion of Mormon soldiers from what is now Utah to San Diego, California to reinforce U.S. troops in California. They began their journey on the Santa Fe Trail and extended the trail as they traveled from Santa Fe all the way to San Diego, California, on the

Pacific Ocean. The Mormon soldiers chopped down trees, dug wells, and cleared away rocks and boulders until they had opened a wagon trail to the Pacific as ordered. They finished the road and reached San Diego on January 29, 1847. Their commander described the accomplishment: "History may be searched in vain for an equal march of infantry. Half of it has been through a wilderness where nothing but savages and wild beasts are found, or deserts where, for want of water, there is no living creature. There, with almost hopeless labor we have dug deep wells . . . marching half naked and half fed, and living upon wild animals, we have discovered and made a road of great value to our country."

▲ A railroad advertisement encouraging travelers to experience history by riding the railroad over old West trails. The first railroad engine drove into Santa Fe in February 1880. A newspaper headline of the day described the event, "The Old Santa Fe Trail Passes Into Oblivion."

End of the Santa Fe Trail

The Mormon Battalion's wagon road proved to be of great value to the country. When gold was discovered in California in 1848, thousands of immigrants and gold seekers used the new route. By the 1880s, however, the Santa Fe and Southern Pacific railroads had built tracks over the old trail, essentially replacing it.

New Mexico and Arizona had prospered by having the trail cross their territory, and new towns were built along the trail to accommodate the thousands of travelers. The population increase brought about by these towns made it possible for New Mexico and Arizona to become states in 1912.

Chapter 4

The Oregon Trail

The Oregon Trail, which stretched for more than 2,000 miles (3,200 km) across North America, was one of the longest and most famous trails of the American West. The trail's length and difficult terrain, however, made it one of the deadliest trails as well, and one out of ten people who began a trip on the trail died along the way.

The trail was officially blazed in 1812, and wagons carrying settlers in search of fertile farming land in the Pacific Northwest first crossed the Oregon Trail in the 1840s. As the only practical way for eastern settlers with wagons to cross the continent and reach the Pacific, its frequent use continued for more than two decades.

◀ An 1860s illustration showing travelers using oxen to pull their wagons on westward trails. The cheaper oxen were favored on the Oregon Trail because grass was plentiful enough to feed them and they were easier to control than mules.

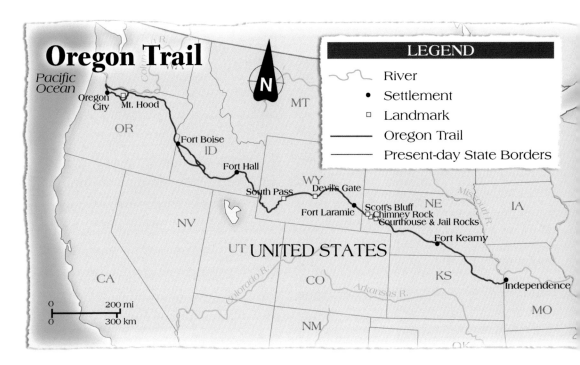

The Route

Towns along the Missouri River, such as St. Louis, St. Joseph, Council Bluffs, and Independence, Missouri, were the jumping-off places for the Oregon Trail. The western trip along the trail took about five months, and travelers began the journey in April or May, so they would have good weather conditions for traveling. Wagon trains leaving too late could be snowbound by winter blizzards in the Rocky Mountains.

The first stage of the trail followed the south bank of the Platte River west through what is now Nebraska and Wyoming. Travelers judged their progress by passing familiar landmarks, such as Jailhouse Rock, Courthouse Rock, Chimney Rock, Scott's Bluff, and Devil's Gate. Travelers could stop for supplies at Fort Kearny in Nebraska and Fort Laramie in eastern Wyoming.

After crossing the South Pass of the Rocky Mountains in Wyoming, the trail sharply angled northwestward, passing Fort

▲ This map traces the route of the Oregon Trail.

23

Hall and Fort Boise as it followed and crossed portions of the Snake and Columbia Rivers in Idaho. Travelers who spotted Mount Hood in the Cascade Mountains knew they were nearing the end of the trail in Oregon City and the Willamette River Valley.

History of the Oregon Trail

The Oregon Trail began as a series of unconnected paths used by Native Americans long before Anglo settlers arrived. Fur traders later began expanding the paths into foot and pack trails to transport pelts. One of these traders, mountain man Robert Stuart, is credited with first crossing the Oregon Trail by foot in 1812 while returning from an expedition funded by the American Fur Company. He and three companions—one who went insane from the difficult journey—crossed the trail

▼ Artist Daniel Jenks also traveled along the Oregon Trail. This sketch shows his wagon traveling by raft on the Platte River. He drew this while camped in central Wyoming in 1859.

in reverse, from Fort Astor in present-day Oregon to St. Louis in Missouri. Stuart was the first to discover the South Pass, but his boss, John Jacob Astor, considered the information so important to the success of his fur trading business that he kept the discovery secret until Jedediah Smith found and told others about the pass in 1824.

After knowledge of the South Pass was released, more people began to explore the Oregon Trail. In 1831, Joseph Reddeford Walker agreed to help Captain Benjamin Louis Eulalie de Bonneville explore. The men traveled along the Platte River, crossed the South Pass, then split to go separate ways at the Great Salt Lake. Bonneville explored a northwest trail toward Oregon, following the Snake and Columbia Rivers. He sent Walker west from Salt Lake and instructed him to explore the western terrain to the Pacific Ocean. Walker did that, becoming the first Anglo to see the Yosemite Valley on his way to the Pacific.

The migration of settlers along the Oregon Trail began to increase in 1836 when missionaries Marcus and Narcissa Whitman became the first to travel across the Oregon Trail in a covered wagon. Then, in 1843, one thousand additional people made the journey to Oregon in one large wagon train of about one hundred twenty wagons to claim farms in the West. This wagon train is known as the "Great Migration," and its success inspired scores of other people to move West, too.

Buffalo along the Trail

When pioneers were crossing the Oregon Trail in the 1800s, huge expanses of open land known as prairies or plains covered the Midwest. Experts today estimate that about 60 million buffalo once roamed this land. Buffalo both helped and hurt travelers on the trail. A stampeding herd of buffalo was danger-

▶ This woman and child are collecting buffalo dung. Travelers burned the pieces of dung, which were popularly called chips, to use as fuel along the trail.

ous and could knock over wagons and trample people. A slowly moving herd could delay the passage of a wagon train. Buffalo, however, provided two important needs—food and fuel. Travelers hunted the animal for food and sport, and, in treeless areas, they collected dried buffalo chips for fuel.

Native Americans along the Trail

The Oregon Trail also crossed the territory of many different Native American groups, including the Cheyenne, Pawnee, Sioux, and Shoshone. Although many travelers feared attacks from Native Americans, and most wagon trains were heavily armed as a result, actual attacks along the Oregon Trail were rare. Many fur traders had already established friendly relationships with the Native Americans in the Pacific Northwest, and American Indians were accustomed to trading and doing business with non-Natives.

In the early years of travel along the Oregon Trail, Native American groups traded horses or food with travelers in exchange for tobacco, clothes, or firearms. For small payments, many Native Americans would help pioneers round up lost cattle, cross rivers, and pull wagons out of the mud.

Relations between travelers and Native Americans worsened, however, as increasing numbers of settlers traveled the trail. They overhunted buffalo, brought livestock that overgrazed the grass, and established settlements in Native American territory. Plains tribes, who depended on the buffalo for survival, found their way of life threatened, and some began scattered attacks on wagon trains to protect their hunting grounds.

The Pacific Northwest

Although some settled along the trail, the great majority of travelers were headed to the Pacific Northwest. The explorations of Lewis and Clark gave the United States a reason to lay a claim to the Pacific Northwest, a region already claimed by Great Britain because of the many British fur traders operating there for the Hudson's Bay Company. To keep peace, Great Britain and the United States had agreed in 1818 to jointly control the area they named Oregon Country, which consisted of what is now Oregon, Washington, Idaho, and portions of Montana, and Wyoming as well as British Columbia, Canada.

The trail opened in the late 1820s, and, by the 1840s, travel along it greatly increased U.S. settlement in the Pacific Northwest. Many U.S. settlers wanted the United States to control the area. Britain and the United States appeared close to declaring war over the contested region, but the countries finally agreed to a compromise in 1846. In the Oregon Treaty, they divided the Pacific Northwest at the 49th parallel; Great Britain owned land north of the 49th parallel. The United States eventually formed the states of Washington, Oregon, and Idaho from the territory.

Chapter 5

The Mormon Trail

The Mormon Trail, also called the Nevada Trail, was the only western trail created for religious reasons. Members of the Church of Jesus Christ of Latter-Day Saints, known as Mormons, blazed the Mormon Trail from what is now Illinois to present-day Utah in 1846 to escape religious persecution in the East. By 1870, about seventy thousand Mormons from around the world had traveled the trail to reach Salt Lake City, Utah. It quickly became a well-traveled route. Hundreds of non-Mormon travelers, traders, and prospectors headed to mineral strikes in Nevada or California crossed the trail.

The Route

The Mormon Trail stretched more than 1,032 miles (1,661 km) from Nauvoo in what is now Illinois to present-day Salt Lake City, Utah. Once

◀ These Mormons of 1912 are reenacting the 1847 trip of the Mormon pioneers on the trail into Mountain Dell.

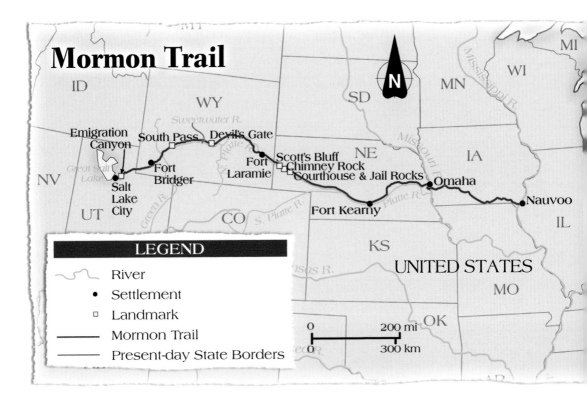

Mormon Trail

ID

WY

Sweetwater R.

Emigration Canyon — South Pass — Devil's Gate

Fort Bridger — Fort Laramie — Scott's Bluff — Chimney Rock — Courthouse & Jail Rocks — Omaha

Great Salt Lake

NV

Salt Lake City

UT

Green R.

CO

S. Platte R.

Fort Kearny

NE

IA

Missouri R.

SD

N

MN

WI

MI

Mississippi R.

Nauvoo

IL

LEGEND

~~ River
• Settlement
□ Landmark
—— Mormon Trail
—— Present-day State Borders

KS

Arkansas R.

UNITED STATES

MO

0   200 mi   **OK**
├─────────┤
0   300 km

through Iowa, the route followed the Oregon Trail's course, but instead of traveling along the south bank of the Platte River, as the Oregon Trail did, the Mormon Trail followed the northern bank of the Platte River through Nebraska and Wyoming.

At Fort Laramie in southeastern Wyoming, the Mormons crossed to the south side of the Platte River and followed the Oregon Trail for a brief time as it veered west to follow the Sweetwater River and across the South Pass of the Rocky Mountains. After crossing South Pass, the Mormon Trail completely broke from the course of the Oregon Trail to travel southwest to Utah across the Green River. The last landmark before Salt Lake City was Emigration Canyon. Mormon representatives from Salt Lake City would often ride there and bring food to greet new arrivals passing through the canyon.

▲ The Mormon Trail crossed four states before it reached Salt Lake City.

History of the Mormon Trail

Followers of the Mormon faith were moving long before the Mormon Trail was blazed. In 1830, Joseph Smith founded the Mormon religion in New York with teachings based on the Bible and the Book of Mormon. Some Mormon teachings at this time, such as allowing men to have more than one wife, angered non-Mormons, and violent mobs drove Smith and his followers from place to place—from Illinois to Missouri to Ohio and back to Illinois. Smith was eventually murdered in 1844, and Mormon leaders named Brigham Young as Smith's successor.

As leader of the Mormons, Young faced a crisis—Mormons were regularly being beaten and killed and their businesses destroyed. Young felt that the only solution was to leave the region east of the Mississippi and move to an unsettled place out West where Mormons could live in peace. To make this dream a reality, Young masterminded one of the largest migrations in history. He planned to lead the faithful Mormons in a search for an as-yet-unknown land God had chosen, which Young named New Zion.

The search for New Zion was hastened in 1845 when the government of Illinois demanded that the Mormons leave Nauvoo—the prosperous city they had founded. To avoid any more bloodshed, Brigham Young instructed Mormons to prepare to evacuate their homes. His Mormon followers packed their belongings in wagons, and beginning on February 4, 1846, sev-

▲ Mormon leader Brigham Young had twenty-seven wives and fifty-seven children. Two of his wives and one of his sons died while staying at Winter Quarters on the Mormons' trip west.

Beat Down and Wore Out

Many of the Mormons kept diaries of their travels on the Mormon Trail to New Zion (Salt Lake City). Oliver Huntington wrote about his experience traveling with a large group of Mormons in 1847.

" I never saw so buisy a thing as in traveling with the Camp—there was hardly ever a minute to spare to read, write or even to pray. As soon as we stoped at any place I had to spring right to my regular daily duties, to get through by bed time. Our daily tasks were regular. As soon as we had struck our wagon in the Corell, unyoke the cattle, gather wood, or Buffalo chips for cooking, and usually to save fuel, dig a hole in the ground about 3 feet long, one wide, and 6 inches deep—this prevented the wind from blowing the heat away—our wood generall being dry, burned well. The next thing was to get the Cow (they were drove all togather clean behind all the company) and milk then drive stakes to tye the Cattle to and about this time the drove would come in and then get the cattle and tie them. There were regular—and sometimes as many more, according to Company ground, Sometimes have to go a mile and a half [2.4 km] for water and sometimes had to dig wells . . . The hurding and guarding togather with my daily tasks, kept me beat down and wore out all the time . . . "

eral thousand men, women, and children left Nauvoo, crossed the Mississippi River, and headed West.

Traveling in the winter snow and sleet was difficult, and the pioneers faced temperatures far below freezing. Illness was common in the cold, wet conditions, and hundreds of Mormons died from typhoid, scurvy, and whooping cough.

The snow made the ground wet and muddy, and wagons frequently stuck in the muck while crossing Iowa's prairies. At night, the Mormons camped in tent cities along the riverbanks. Along the route, Young left selected Mormons to form new settlements in Iowa, such as Garden Grove and Mount Pisgah. These Mormons stayed and dug wells, built bridges, and established ferries to help future Mormon travelers across creeks and rivers. About 16,000 Mormons made the trip across Iowa in 1846 and established Winter Headquarters in what is now Florence, Nebraska. By the winter of 1847, the main group of Mormons reached

Winter Headquarters. They built more than six hundred dwellings out of sod or logs and stayed there until spring.

While camped in Winter Headquarters, Young organized a Pioneer Company of about one hundred forty-eight people who would journey from Winter Headquarters to find New Zion. Then, they would return and lead the rest of the group to their new home.

In April 1847, Young set out with the Pioneer Company and about seventy-two wagons full of supplies and livestock. Their day began with a bugle call at 5 A.M., and the wagons rotated position so that no one would always have to ride in the dusty rear position. Young gave special duties to each pioneer—marking the trail, posting signs with estimated mileage, improving the road by clearing it of boulders and stumps, hunting wild game, or guard duty.

The group followed the north bank of the Platte River for more than 800 miles (1,287 km), making several dangerous river crossings, then hiked across the Rocky Mountains through the South Pass. While crossing the mountains, Young became ill and had to ride the rest of the way in a wagon. When he saw the Great Salt Lake Valley from the back of the wagon, he confirmed that it was New Zion. "This is the right place," he said. "Drive on!"

On July 21, 1847, the Pioneer Company began to settle in the Great Salt Lake Valley. Mormons began building irrigation ditches and new houses immediately upon their arrival. Farmers planted acres of potatoes, corn, buckwheat, beans, and oats. Young was kept busy mapping the plan for a temple and the city of Salt Lake.

New Mormon settlers began arriving in Salt Lake City after following the Pioneer Company's tracks. By August 1847, about

◀ A Mormon family, pictured on the trail in about 1870. The biggest hazard for pioneer families on the trail was not broken-down wagons, conflicts with Indians, or even bad weather, but disease. Cholera, a highly contagious bacterial infection that thrives in unsanitary conditions, killed thousands of pioneers on their way west.

four hundred fifty Mormons were living in Salt Lake. That month, Young left the new settlement to return to Winter Headquarters and led the rest of the group to "New Zion." The settlement quickly grew, and more than five thousand Mormons lived in Salt Lake City by the end of 1848.

End of the Mormon Trail

The Mormon Trail dramatically increased the population of Utah. In 1850, Congress created the Utah Territory, which included all but the tip of present-day Nevada. Most of the settlers in the Utah Territory were Mormons. Mormon-founded Salt Lake City was named the capital of the Utah Territory in the mid-1850s, and Young served as its first territorial governor until 1857.

The Mormon Trail proved so popular that the Pony Express—a fast relay system of mail delivery created in 1860 to quickly bring mail from Missouri through the Rocky Mountains to California—built stations along the Mormon Trail and used its route. Most people stopped using the Mormon Trail after the Transcontinental Railroad was completed in 1869.

Chapter 6

The California Trail

The California Trail from Missouri through Kansas, Wyoming, and Nevada was the most-traveled trail to the West, thanks, in part, to articles in newspapers around the world that chronicled the wonders of California. As an article in The *Saint Louis Weekly Reveille* declared to its readers, "There is no country holding forth such great inducements to emigrants as California . . . a soil unsurpassed for richness and productiveness . . . the gold, silver and precious gems that the earth is holding in its flinty bosom, and which, in some cases, nature has so exposed as to render them available without the cost of labor and expense." Lured by these dreams of the paradise of California, an estimated two hundred thousand people crossed the California Trail between 1840 and 1860.

◄ Travelers ride through Yosemite Valley on the California Trail in this 1889 illustration. Joe Walker, a mountain man, was the first to explore the Yosemite Valley. There, he and his men became the first Anglos to see the huge redwood trees known as Sequoias.

Route of the California Trail

At its start, the California Trail followed the Oregon Trail from its jumping-off towns in Missouri, across the Kansas prairies, and over the South Pass of the Rocky Mountains in what is now Wyoming. After crossing the Rockies, travelers found themselves at the Parting of the Ways where the Oregon branch of the trail traveled northwest and the California branch of the trail stretched southwest through Nevada.

The main California Trail passed Soda Springs in present-day Idaho, then continued southwest into Nevada. Travelers could also choose the Hastings Cutoff, which bypassed Soda Springs to stop at Fort Bridger in present-day Wyoming and cross what is now Utah.

The Hastings Cutoff rejoined the main trail in Nevada to follow the Humboldt River. Along the Humboldt River, travel-

▼ This map shows the route of the California Trail.

35

ers dealt with poor water, dust clouds, lack of food, and steep canyons. The route also crossed Native American lands, and sometimes Indians, or bandits pretending to be Indians, attacked wagon trains.

After passing through Nevada, settlers had to cross the Sierra Nevada Mountains to enter California. They could not stop and rest long because they had to be across the mountains by October 1, or risk becoming stuck in the snowy mountain passes. Any livestock too tired to keep up with the wagon train was cut loose and left to take care of itself. An 1850 report described nine thousand seven hundred dead animal carcasses and about three thousand wagons littering the sides of the trail through Nevada.

Once in California, the trail passed Sutter's Fort and ended at Sacramento or Yerba Buena (present-day San Francisco).

History of the California Trail

The California Trail was first blazed in 1833 by a group of sixty-five trappers led by Joseph Reddeford Walker. The first group of settlers to cross Nevada to California is generally considered to be the Bartelson-Bidwell Party, which made the trip in 1841. They abandoned their wagons along the way, however, believing the Sierra Nevada Mountains too steep to ride across.

In 1844, Elisha Stephens's group was the first to move some wagons across the Sierra Nevada Mountains. They left Council Bluffs, Iowa, on May 18, 1844, with eleven wagons drawn by teams of oxen. They followed the established trail along the Platte River and over the South Pass of the Rockies. From the Sink of the Humboldt River, the team blazed a new portion of the trail, known as the Truckee Route, past Truckee Lake and through Truckee Pass in California (in 1847 renamed Donner Lake and Donner Pass). To get their wagons through the pass,

◀ These wagons are making their way through Donner Pass over the Sierra Nevada Mountain in the mid-1800s. Several years earlier, blizzards trapped a group of travelers that have come to be known as the Donner Party, in this pass.

they unloaded items in 2-foot (.6-meter) deep snowdrifts and carried their goods by hand to the summit of the mountain. Then, they unhitched the livestock and led the oxen one by one through a narrow path through the next set of rock walls. The oxen were hitched to the wagons at the top of the path, and the wagons were pulled slowly over a third rock wall. They then smoothly descended the western slope of the mountain to the Sacramento Valley.

The Donner Party

In 1846, George Donner organized a group to travel to California along the trail and recruited members by advertising in the Springfield, Illinois, *Gazette*: "Who wants to go to California without costing them anything? As many as eight young men of good character who can drive an ox team will be accommodated. Come, boys, you can have as much land as you want without costing you anything."

Hungry Times

Patrick Breen was one of the survivors of the Donner Party. He kept a journal of his family's experiences in camp.

" Friday Nov. 20th 1846. Came to this place on the 31st of 1846 last month that it snowed we went on to the pass the snow so deep we were unable to find the road, when within 3 miles [5 km] of the summit then turned back to this shanty on the Lake, Stanton came one day after we arriveed here we again took our teams & waggons & made another unsuccessful attempt to cross in company with Stanton we returned to the shanty it continueing to snow all the time we were here we now have killed most part of our cattle having to stay here untill next spring & live on poor beef without bread or salt

December 1st Tuesday Still snowing wind W snow about 5 1/2 feet or 6 deep difficult to get wood no going from the house completely housed up looks as likely for snow as when it commenced, our cattle all killed but three or four them, the horses & Stantons mules gone & cattle suppose lost in the snow no hopes of finding them alive.

Mond. 21 Milt. got back last night from Donos camp sad news. Jake Donno Sam Shoemaker Rinehart, & Smith are dead the rest of them in a low situation Snowed all night with a strong S-W wind to day cloudy wind continues but not snowing, thawing sun shineing dimly in hopes it will clear off.

Wens. 13th Snowing fast wind N.W snow higher than the shanty must be 13 feet deep dont know how to get wood this morning it is dredful to look at.

Thursd. 21 Fine morning wind W did not freze quite so hard last night as it has done, John Battice & Denton came this morning with Eliza she wont eat hides Mrs Reid sent her back to live or die on them. Milt. got his toes froze the Donoghs are all well.

Thursd. 25th Froze hard last night fine & sunshiny to day wind W. Mrs Murphy says the wolves are about to dig up the dead bodies at her shanty, the nights are too cold to watch them, we hear them howl.

Mond. 8th Fine clear morning wind S. W. froze hard last. Spitzer died last night about 3 o clock to we will bury him in the snow Mrs Eddy died on the night of the 7th.

Frid 26th Froze hard last night today clear & warm Wind S: E: blowing briskly Marthas jaw swelled with the toothache; hungry times in camp, plenty hides but the folks will not eat them we eat them with a tolerable good apetite. Thanks be to Almighty God. Amen Mrs Murphy said here yesterday that thought she would commence on Milt. & eat him. I dont that she has done so yet, it is distressing The Donnos told the California folks that they commence to eat the dead people 4 days ago, if they did not succeed that day or next in finding their cattle then under ten or twelve feet of snow & did not know the spot or near it, I suppose they have done so ere this time. "

Several families replied to Donner's ad, and that spring, Donner led a party of men, women, and children from Springfield, Illinois, toward California. Several delays along the trail, such as waiting to cross flooded rivers, meant that the party would be crossing the Sierra Nevada Mountains late in the season.

The wagon train's worst mistake was in choosing to take the Hastings Cutoff, a new, untried shortcut through Utah that crossed more difficult terrain than the usual trail. The party had to clear the trail of trees and bush so wagons could pass. They reached Truckee Pass in late October and stopped in the pass just 3 miles (5 km) short of the mountain summit to rest for several days because they had no energy to cross it. Before they could cross to the westward side, a blizzard trapped them in the pass, and they were forced to spend the winter there.

During the winter of 1846 to 1847, they faced huge snow-falls and below-freezing temperatures. They ran out of food and fuel. Thirty-nine of the eighty-seven members of the Donner Party died of cold or starvation before spring, and to stay alive some survivors were forced to eat people who had died.

Gold Rush

An accidental discovery in California in 1848 eventually made the California Trail the most popular thoroughfare in the West. On January 24, a carpenter named James Marshall saw gold shining in the American River at Sutter's Mill near San Francisco.

After gold was discovered, newspaper stories described the strike as being so rich that gold was lying on the ground for people to pick up with no effort. These stories convinced people from all parts of the world to journey to California to search for riches. Some of the first to arrive were about ninety thousand prospectors—known as forty-niners—who flooded the area in 1849. Many of them traveled to California from the Eastern United States along the California Trail.

Chapter 7

End of the Trails

The golden era of westward trails lasted from about 1803 to 1869. During these years, routes were continuously improved and turned into stagecoach routes and Federal Wagon Roads.

As new technology spread across the West, however, the use of trails came to an end. The railroads built thousands of miles of tracks, and, for the first time in history, a cheap, relatively safe, and quick way to transport people and supplies to western areas existed. Many railroad lines, such as the Santa Fe, built tracks directly over the old dirt trails, thus replacing them forever.

Railroads

Although well-blazed trails served to open the West to settlement, travel on them was slow and dangerous. U.S.

◀ An 1867 picture of Central Pacific Railroad workers riding a supply train carrying wood for building track. They are in the Bloomer Cut, a corridor constructed through the Sierra Nevada Mountains for the Transcontinental Railroad.

◀ People began transporting covered wagons by train to their desired destinations. In this 1914 picture, U.S. military troops are unloading their wagons in Colorado.

leaders in favor of westward expansion knew that the best way to encourage settlement and trade was to create faster, improved transportation routes across the country. Beginning in the 1850s, the government hired surveyors to plan the best route for a railroad to link the East and West Coasts of the United States.

In 1862, Congress passed the Pacific Railroad Act, which authorized funding for a Transcontinental Railroad to link all sections of the country. To fund the construction, Congress gave loans and millions of acres of free land grants to the Union Pacific and the Central Pacific railroad companies. Railroads, to finance their construction work, then sold the land to settlers.

The Union Pacific Railroad began construction working west from present-day Omaha, Nebraska, and the Central Pacific Railroad worked east from what is now Sacramento, California. Thousands of workers—mainly African Americans

▶ Railroad owners and workers as well as politicians celebrate the completion of the transcontinental railroad in 1867.

and Chinese and European immigrants—worked to clear the land and build the tracks. The tracks met on May 10, 1869, at Promontory Summit in Utah Territory. To commemorate the joining of the Transcontinental Railroad, railroad owners drove a golden spike into the ground to join both sections of the 1,774-mile (2,855-km) long track.

The U.S. government went on to fund other transcontinental railroads. The second one, linking the Southern Pacific Railroad with the Atchison, Topeka, and Santa Fe Railroad, finished on March 8, 1881, in New Mexico. In 1893, the privately funded and constructed Great Northern Railway, passing through Minnesota, the Dakotas, Montana, Utah, Washington, and Oregon, opened for business.

Hundreds of thousands of settlers had risked the trip by trail, but as even more settlers came West with the railroad, new towns formed along railroad stops to meet the settlers' needs.

◀ This diverse crew includes African American, Anglo, and Chinese American railroad workers. They are resting on a transportation cart while laying track for the Central Pacific Railroad in the 1860s.

▼ This map traces the route of the transcontinental railroads.

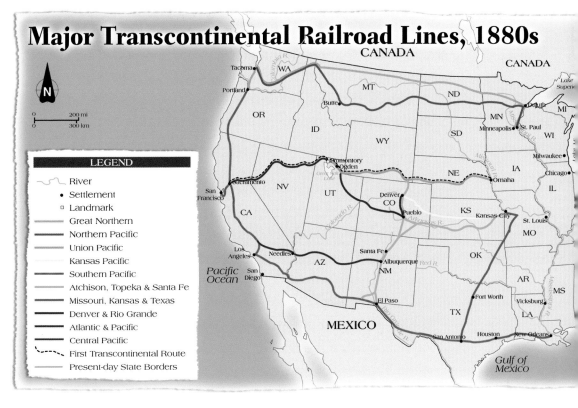

Major Transcontinental Railroad Lines, 1880s

LEGEND

- ～ River
- • Settlement
- ▫ Landmark
- Great Northern
- Northern Pacific
- Union Pacific
- Kansas Pacific
- Southern Pacific
- Atchison, Topeka & Santa Fe
- Missouri, Kansas & Texas
- Denver & Rio Grande
- Atlantic & Pacific
- Central Pacific
- First Transcontinental Route
- Present-day State Borders

▶ These men are camping while following a trail to Pike's Peak, Colorado.

Western trails helped the United States to achieve Manifest Destiny by enabling the transportation of settlers, supplies, and goods to new areas in the West. Trails increased trade opportunities between western and eastern regions, and the U.S. economy prospered as territories became interdependent on each other for goods.

In the process, settlers from different regions of the country intermingled, and regional loyalties began to be replaced by a new feeling of nationalism. People began to think of themselves as Americans—working together to build a nation.

Not all the effects of settling the frontier were positive, however. The influx of Anglo settlers caused the destruction of the Native American lifestyle. To clear the way for settlement, the United States broke treaties, took Native American land, and harshly imposed U.S. government on Native groups.

Like the government, settlers too were convinced of their Manifest Destiny and went to great lengths to fulfill that "destiny." People made the long, dangerous trek on western trails in search of the American dream of a better life. For some, the trip resulted in triumphs, but for others the trail's end brought heartache or death. Regardless of the individual outcome, the travelers of the famous trails west forever changed the landscape of the American West.

1803: ▶ The United States doubles its size with land bought in the Louisiana Purchase.

1812: ▶ Robert Stuart first discovers South Pass through the Rocky Mountains.

1821: ▶ Merchandise caravans first begin using the Santa Fe Trail.

1823: ▶ President James Monroe declares American intentions of expansion in a speech known as the Monroe Doctrine.

1830: ▶ Congress passes the Indian Removal Act, legalizing the removal and resettlement of Native American groups.

1841: ▶ First settlers arrive in California via the California Trail.

1843: ▶ Great Migration occurs along the Oregon Trail.

1844: ▶ First wagons cross the Sierra Nevada Mountains while traveling to California.

1845: ▶ Texas becomes a state.

1846: ▶ Mexican-American War begins; General Kearny marches troops along the Santa Fe Trail and takes over New Mexico; Mormon Battalion completes military supply road from Santa Fe to San Diego; Mormons blaze the Mormon Trail from Illinois to Salt Lake City, Utah.

1848: ▶ January 24—James Marshall finds gold at Sutter's Mill.
February 2—Mexican-American War ends when Treaty of Guadalupe Hidalgo is signed.

1850: ▶ California becomes a state.

1853: ▶ The United States buys more land from Mexico in the Gadsden Purchase.

1860: ▶ The Pony Express begins delivering mail.

1862: ▶ The Homestead Act—granting free land to settlers who farm and improve it for five years—becomes law.

1864: ▶ Nevada becomes a state.

1867: ▶ United States buys Alaska from Russia.

1869: ▶ The Transcontinental Railroad is completed.

1880: ▶ The Santa Fe Railroad reaches Santa Fe, New Mexico.

1887: ▶ Native American traditional homelands are eliminated when Congress passes the Dawes Act.

1889: ▶ U.S. government opens land in the Indian Territory for non-Indian settlement.

1898: ▶ United States annexes Hawaii.

1900: ▶ Hawaii becomes a U.S. territory.

1907: ▶ Oklahoma becomes a state.

1912: ▶ New Mexico and Arizona become states.

1976: ▶ Homestead Act is repealed.

frontier: edge of known or settled land

manifest: obviously true and easily recognizable. The term Manifest Destiny meant that the true and obvious destiny of the United States was to expand its borders to the Pacific Ocean

migration: mass movement of animals or people from one place to another

Mormon: a member of the Mormon Church; in this sense, also called Latter-day Saint

natural resources: naturally occurring minerals—such as wood, oil, and gold—that can be used or sold, or geographical features such as a good harbor or climate

persecution: The act or practice of persecuting on the basis of race, religion, sexual orientation, or beliefs that differ from those of the persecutor

poverty: the state of being poor; lack of the means of providing material needs or comforts

prospector: person who explores an area looking for mineral resources

rendezvous: a meeting at a prearranged time and place; trappers and traders met once yearly to exchange pelts for money and supplies

rutted: having sunken tracks or grooves made by the passage of vehicles, such as wagons

scurvy: a disease caused by deficiency of vitamin C, characterized by spongy and bleeding gums, bleeding under the skin, and extreme weakness

smallpox: An acute, highly infectious, often fatal disease caused by a poxvirus and characterized by high fever and aches with subsequent widespread eruption of pimples that blister, produce pus, and form pockmarks

stagecoach: a four-wheeled horse-drawn vehicle formerly used to transport mail, parcels, and passengers over a regular route

strike: discovery of gold or other precious metal.

trapper: hunter who uses traps to kill animals such as beaver or squirrel for their fur.

typhoid fever: a life-threatening illness with a high fever caused by the bacterium *Salmonella typhi*

Books

Cook, Diane. *Pathfinders of the American Frontier: the Men Who Opened the Frontier of North America, from Daniel Boone and Alexander Mackenzie to Lewis and Clark and Zebulon Pike.* Philadelphia: Mason Crest, 2003.

Hamilton, John. *To the Pacific.* Edina, Minn.: Abdo & Daughters, 2003.

King, David. *American Voices: Westward Expansion.* New York: John Wiley & Sons, 2003.

Long, Cathryn J. *Westward Expansion.* San Diego: Kidhaven Press, 2003.

Uschan, Michael V. *The Oregon Trail.* Landmark Events in American History (series). Milwaukee: World Almanac® Library, 2004.

Uschan, Michael V. *The Transcontinental Railroad.* Landmark Events in American History (series). Milwaukee: World Almanac® Library, 2004.

Wadsworth, Ginger. *Words West: Voices of Young Pioneers.* New York: Clarion Books, 2003.

Web Sites

California National Historic Trail
http://www.nps.gov/cali/

Homestead Act
http://www.nps.gov/home/homestead_act.html

Mountain Men and the Fur Trade
www.xmission.com/~drudy/amm.html

Museum of Westward Expansion
www.nps.gov/jeff/expansion_museum.html

National Oregon/California Trail Center
http://www.oregontrailcenter.org/

The Oregon Trail
http://www.isu.edu/%7Etrinmich/Oregontrail.html